THE NEW CULT OF
EFFICIENCY AND EDUCATION

HORACE MANN LECTURE
1968

THE NEW CULT OF
EFFICIENCY AND EDUCATION

BY

H. THOMAS JAMES

Dean, School of Education, Stanford University

LIBRARY OF CONGRESS CATALOG
Card Number 69-12331

HORACE MANN LECTURES

PUBLIC EDUCATION
AND A PRODUCTIVE SOCIETY
By Maurice J. Thomas, 1953
$2.95s

THE SCHOOL
THAT BUILT A NATION
By Joy Elmer Morgan, 1954
(Out of Print)

THE EDUCATION OF FREE MEN
By Ernest O. Melby, 1955
(Out of Print)

EDUCATION FACES
NEW DEMANDS
By Francis S. Chase, 1956
$2.95s

FISCAL READINESS
FOR THE STRESS OF CHANGE
By Paul R. Mort, 1957
(Out of Print)

FACTORS THAT INFLUENCE
LEARNING
By Daniel A. Prescott, 1958
(Out of Print)

THE DISCIPLINE OF EDUCATION
AND AMERICA'S FUTURE
By Lawrence D. Haskew, 1959
(Out of Print)

PSYCHOLOGY OF THE CHILD
IN THE MIDDLE CLASS
By Allison Davis, 1960
$2.95s

PERSONNEL POLICIES
FOR PUBLIC EDUCATION
By Francis Keppel, 1961
$2.95s

EDUCATION AND THE
FOUNDATIONS OF HUMAN FREEDOM
By George S. Counts, 1962
$2.95s

A DESIGN FOR TEACHER
EDUCATION
By Paul H. Masoner, 1963
$2.95s

CRITICAL ISSUES IN
AMERICAN PUBLIC EDUCATION
By John K. Norton, 1964
$2.95s

THE GENIUS
OF AMERICAN EDUCATION
By Lawrence A. Cremin, 1965
$2.95s

SOCIAL PROBLEMS IN
PUBLIC SCHOOL ADMINISTRATION
By Benjamin C. Willis, 1966
$2.95s

PRESIDENTIAL STATEMENTS
ON EDUCATION
Compiled by Maurice J. Thomas, 1967
$2.95s

THE TEACHER
AND THE MACHINE
By Philip W. Jackson, 1967
$2.95s

THE NEW CULT OF EFFICIENCY
AND EDUCATION
By H. Thomas James, 1968
$2.95s

THE HORACE MANN LECTURESHIP

To commemorate the life of Horace Mann, 1796–1859, and in recognition of his matchless services to the American Public School System, the School of Education of the University of Pittsburgh, in cooperation with the Tri-State Area School Study Council, established the Horace Mann Lectureship. The striking and varied contributions of Horace Mann must ever be kept alive and be reemphasized in each generation. It is difficult, indeed, to assess the magnitude of Mann's educational services. Turning from the profession of law, he devoted his life to the study and improvement of education. He, more than any other, can truly be called "Father of the American Public School System." His boundless energy, coupled with a brilliant and penetrating mind, focused the attention of the citizens of his era on the need for the improvement and support of public schools. His services were manifold. It shall be the purpose of these Lectures to reaffirm his faith in free schools and to call to their service all citizens of this generation. It is vital that all understand the purpose and function of a free public school system in American Democracy.

HORACE MANN LECTURE
1968

The New Cult of
Efficiency and Education

M ODERN man is preoccupied with the machine. Rare indeed is the human being today who spends much of his waking life away from the sights and sounds of machinery at work in the car, the tractor, or the airplane, and in heat or water-pumping machines or electric generators which can be heard from pole to pole, even in Eskimo villages, in desert oases, and on remote South Sea islands. It is perhaps not surprising that in an age of preoccupation with the machine, man finds it congenial to describe his social institutions in mechanistic terms. As we build complex machines to travel the sea, the land, the air, or outer space, and build within them complex subsystems for heating and cooling,

1

for processing air, for sanitation, for feeding, and entertaining, we build models and develop language and habits of thought that become plausible and perhaps useful for describing our social institutions as well. We are accustomed to testing the output of our machines in precise units of miles per hour traveled or other equally precise terms, and grow quickly irritable when they fail to perform precisely within the small tolerances we allow them. Similarly we enter knowledgeably and enthusiastically into conversations about how to correct or improve the performance of our machines by noting precisely the variations from the standards we expect. We understand and on occasion offer to supervise the processes for correcting or improving a machine: how to check back along its complex subsystems to all the inputs to see where we can substitute new, repaired, or cheaper parts that will reduce the inputs, or increase the outputs, in order to improve efficiency. Those who come to follow this pattern of thought find it easy, guided by the criterion of efficiency, to apply the same kind of analyses to our social institutions as well, even to schools.

It is difficult in these times to recognize how unstructured the planning for school expenditures was early in this century. Few schools made any serious attempt to forecast or budget for expenditures, and what planning was done was sporadic, inconsequential, and nonuniform among schools.

Two events in 1911 began the movement toward more uniformity and specificity in school budgeting and accounting. The first was an effort by the U. S. Office of Education to standardize accounting for schools— one of a long series of efforts that have recurred each decade since. The other was the publication of *The Principles of Scientific Management* by Frederick W. Taylor, which stressed the need to find the best way to work, and which placed responsibility for this task on management. Subsequently, Henri Fayol in France gave further emphasis to the task of management as the chief executive's work. His efforts to develop a theory of administrative science have had powerful influences on improvement in management in all institutions. He emphasized the need for planning, organization, and for command, cooperation, and control.

All of these early efforts emphasized technical efficiency. It is not surprising that their heavy emphasis on rationality resulted in neglect of the human relations aspect of administration. Eventually, there was a cycle of withdrawal from the concerns of technical efficiency, a movement marked by the work of Elton Mayo in the late 1920's at the Hawthorn Plant of the Western Electric Plant in Chicago. Mayo's studies showed that efficiency could be increased by better human relations with employees. This interest in human relations has persisted ever since and is perhaps best exemplified in the work of F. J. Roethlisberger and William J. Dickson, *Management and the Worker,* published in 1950.

A new emphasis on efficiency grew out of the 1946 Hoover Report on efficiency in government. Subsequently, the development of operations research, general systems theory, and cybernetics stirred renewed interest in the criterion of efficiency. Perhaps the most influential publication in recent years is that of Charles J. Hitch and Roland N. McKean, *The Economics of Defense in the Nuclear Age* (1961), which reveals the sophisticated approaches to efficiency undertaken for the U. S. Department of Defense. Since that time, renewed efforts have proliferated to analyze the operations of other social institutions in ways that permit the application of the criterion of efficiency.

The notion that social institutions can be explained in mechanistic terms is not new, nor confined to modern man, for many of the ancients looked for the same regularities in the affairs of man that they found in the physical and mathematical sciences. The great burst of scientific progress in the seventeenth century spurred renewed efforts to explain social institutions in the dependable terms of physical, mathematical, and mechanical relationships. In our time, the impact of engineering and operations analysis on the administration of schools early in the the century has been remarkable. Raymond Callahan's conclusions have raised serious questions about the appropriateness of many of these applications, and his book is replete with illustrations of ineptness in their use.[1]

More recently a newer priesthood of econ-

[1] Raymond E. Callahan, *Education and the Cult of Efficiency* (Chicago: University of Chicago Press, 1962).

omists and political scientists has joined the
engineers in advising government about improving schools, and schoolmen now have a
new catechism to learn. Increasingly, state
and national lawmakers are asking economists
and political scientists for new solutions to
old problems in education; and as government makes the study of education both
popular and profitable, the number of re-
searchers from these disciplines that are interested in education is increasing. The
models they use are, like those of the engineers, adapted from among those long used
to describe physical, mathematical, and mechanical relationships. The direction of their
inquiries and their early conclusions are
changing our ideas about education, as well
as changing our educational institutions, and
perhaps their goals.

*   *   *

There appear to be four general models
especially popular in these new inquiries into
educational matters. These are: (1) the
investment model, in which educational expenditures are analyzed as investments that

result in predictable returns to our economy; in this model man is the machine, schooling is the input, and the output is the product of work that can be aggregated into the gross national product; (2) the *production model,* in which the school is the machine, educational expenditures is an input, and the output is a valuable consumer good (which is a traditional form of analysis, and the one most common to educators; or the output may be analyzed in terms of manpower needs and supply, again a traditional form); (3) the *motivation research model,* which leads to the search for unexpressed needs in a clientele, the development of a product to satisfy the latent need, and a program for "engineering consensus" to arouse popular demand for the product; and (4) the *systems model,* in which the management of schools is analyzed in terms of efficiency, through cost-benefit studies, systems analysis, and program planning and budgeting systems.

All four of these lines of inquiry, and their associated methods of analysis, are influential for they are based on disciplined ways of understanding and they communicate well to people accustomed to similar logic in commerce and industry. Because of their power, they influence the way we restate the aims of education, and the means for achieving those aims. Since they are important, I will comment further on each of the models.

In the first model, education is viewed as an investment in people, with a predictable and very high rate of return to the economy. Some very sophisticated analyses of rates of return to educational investment have developed from the work done at the University of Chicago by Theodore Schultz and his students, notably Gary Becker, now a professor at Columbia University.[2] One of the niceties of Becker's work was his effort to reduce the incredibly high rates of return to educational investment by including on the investment side the cost of earnings foregone by those pursuing an education. Even so, the returns to investment in education, as estimated by studies now replicated many times both here and abroad, remain remarkably high, on the

[2] Theodore W. Schultz, *The Economic Value of Education* (New York: Columbia University Press, 1963).

order of 35 percent for elementary education, 15 percent for higher education, and perhaps 12 percent for advanced graduate study. These studies change the traditional view of school costs as a burden on the taxpayer, or parent, leading us instead to consider various enlightened ways of managing investment in education so as to increase the returns.

It takes no great leap of the imagination, for instance, to move from Miller's analysis of census data, showing very large differences in estimates for individual lifetime income when ordered by levels of education, to conclude that increasing levels of education probably would tend to increase income.[3] Similarly, no great imaginative effort is required to move from estimates of individual income at various levels of education to expectations that aggregations of higher educated individuals by communities, states, and nations could be expected to produce higher aggregates of income also.

[3] Herman P. Miller, "Annual and Lifetime Income in Relation to Education," *American Economic Review,* L (December 1960), pp. 962–86.

Further, this model leads us to examine opportunities often foregone, such as investments in education that reduce the costs of welfare and protective services in our society and throughout the world. If a person drawing welfare benefits can become self-supporting by acquiring an education, society benefits not only by the reduction of welfare costs but also in some measure by the increment the person adds to the total product of goods and services, including the taxes he pays. Likewise, if a prisoner by acquiring an education, can be released to become a productive worker, the double gains of reduced prison costs and increased production benefit society.

Despite its wide appeal, there are those who deplore this materialistic view of education, for not every prospect pleases from this perspective. For instance, it violates Immanuel Kant's categorical imperative, that man is to be viewed as an end in himself, and never as a means to an end. The investment model is associated with such unhappy terms as "human resources," and with ideas about their development, management, and exploitation that horrify some people. In the discussion of ideas generated by this model, we hear less of the aims of education being to free the individual for understanding himself, his world, and his moral and civic responsibilities, and more about manpower training, developing human resource, and improving its usefulness in the pursuit of government- and corporate-defined purposes.

Anyone accustomed to thinking of man as an inquiring and freedom-seeking individual must experience some alarm at the influence of the investment model on our educational institutions, particularly as it encourages the precision with which our colleges and universities are shaping students into identical sets of replaceable units to fit similar sets of institutional roles. The *Dictionary of Occupational Titles* becomes the shopping list for new colleges and universities wanting to define their aims of education; and government licensing agents, or personnel officers in the public or private sector, apply their precise measurements for selecting or rejecting the products of the school, thereby making its degree of success or failure dependent on conformity to their standards. The schools thus become sorters and processors of men to meet the increasingly precise specifications designed by and serving the needs of government and corporations. While details of specifications vary, the whole output of schools becomes characterized by commonalities of deference, obedience, loyalty, and a capacity to look interested in a conversation while thinking about something else.

In time, schools find their place in a hierarchy of prestige that depends on records for placing students in relation to a similar hierarchy of job prestige in the organizations served by the schools. If one were to project this trend, one might foresee the day when the most prestigious school would become a completely closed system, where only faculty children could enter, and the only proper place for its graduates would be appointment to the faculty of that school; and the least prestigious school would have no clients because it would not accept even the children of its own faculty, or hire its own graduates.

One might expect that the revolutionary force necessary to change such a system would come from the accumulating mass of rejects; and indeed, we see, in the increasing restiveness of racial minorities largely excluded from both schooling and employment opportunities, evidence that it does. Not anticipated, however, was the remarkable restiveness now rising to a crescendo among the children of the successful products of the system, of those who had gone to the prestigious schools and met the criteria for the prestigious jobs, and then begot a generation of rebels now engaged in defying the system and demanding that it be changed.

Schools serving all ages now find themselves beset on the one hand by external demands for admission of racial minorities and the poor, who see schooling as the means of entry to the good life as we currently define it, and on the other hand by internal demands from the children of the establishment, who want to change the system in ways that will end the domination of corporately-defined goals and the emphasis on subordinating the individual to collective aims, and who want to restore the view of education as a liberating influence serving individual needs and enhancing the dignity of man.

The general public is becoming more sophisticated and articulate in stating its demands for education. People are no longer willing to serve as the instrumental means of industry—they want to be treated as ultimate ends and to have education directed toward that goal. Industry has not always assumed the responsibility for retraining workers who become obsolete or are displaced by automation, and the common man has learned the lesson of overreliance on specialization. The United Kingdom's Crowther Report in 1959 noted that an important factor transforming the role of education was the importance of being qualified. The report stressed that "being qualified" was a *conditional* demand for an education that would meet the individual's needs, qualify him for a broad spectrum of skills, and provide him with an attested standard of general education.

On balance, the investment model can

produce more sophisticated popular attitudes toward spending money for education as a profitable individual and social investment, but leaves us with some nagging concerns about how it affects the dignity of man, and about materialism as a major goal for humanity.

The production model, in which educational services are viewed as a consumer good produced by the school, is nearest to the view of education held by schoolmen, in the sense that schools are operated to serve the expectations of the community, or, more bluntly, that the local administrator satisfies local demands for education or loses his job. Callahan has emphasized that this fact has made schoolmen peculiarly vulnerable to the demands of businessmen who insist on efficiency.[4] The systematic analysis of schools viewed through the production model is perhaps giving us a clearer understanding of the demands being made on the schools, not only by the local community, but by the nation as well. As this understanding grows, we may expect more local administrators to

[4] Callahan, *op. cit.*, pp. 52–54.

identify more cosmopolitan vision with en-lightened self-interest, and to set about ordering priorities for education in ways that will satisfy larger reference groups than those to be found in their immediate jurisdiction. On the other hand, it should be a matter of broad social concern that the vulnerability of local administrators, and, to a lesser degree, teachers as well, virtually guarantees that the mechanistic models for describing the school will be constantly reinforced by a curriculum designed to produce new and more sophisticated users of these models to describe physical and social phenomena.

The production model for schools also guides manpower studies, which have yet to demonstrate much power for prediction. The reasons for the poor showing of man-power studies are complex but some of the more important can be mentioned. One is that increasing the levels of education in-creases the options the individual has for employment, and since better educated peo-ple substitute for the less educated across all fields of employment with no known ceil-ing, collectively defined manpower needs may not be met simply by raising educational levels—for individuals, unless coerced, will select among their increased options to satisfy their personal needs and not the collectively defined manpower needs.

Nevertheless, such studies played a part in improving guidance and vocational education programs, in attuning the vocational programs of the schools to employment opportunities more broadly defined than the local labor market, and are improving outside funding for local efforts aimed at meeting the larger national needs for a better educated labor force. They also reinforce the demands on the schools to serve the needs of institutions, such as governmental, industrial, and commercial enterprises, rather than individual human needs. One can continue to ponder the widespread popular disinterest in vocational training, not only in this country but around the world, both among the middle and upper classes, who refuse to allow their children to enter vocational training programs, and also among the lower classes, who seem to suspect a conspiracy to keep them serving institutional rather than individually defined purposes.

The third model I mentioned, the motivation research model, is less widely used outside the private sector, and it is not yet clear what its implications are for educational institutions, except that it is currently of interest to those who are attentive to possibilities for production of technological innovations in education. Perhaps it would be more correct to say that the motivation research model is of more interest to those companies that have overproduced products for special clients, notably the military and space agencies of government, and would like to create a market in the schools for existing or anticipated surpluses of their products. Thus business moves from its traditional position of satisfying a demand for goods, to its new position of creating a demand for its products. One need only contemplate the enormous expenditures now being made to sell essentially equal brands of tobacco, soap, aspirin, airline services, and cars to fear for the future of education when the big combinations of corporations and government agencies now forming begin to "engineer consensus" about what products must be bought to educate the young.

The systems model, representing the fourth set of interests—those related to efficiency through cost-benefit studies, systems analysis, and program planning and budgeting systems—promises perhaps the greatest changes for schools through new federal approaches to school financing under the Elementary and Secondary Education Act of 1965, and, in many states, will bring increasing pressures at the state level as well. The new emphasis on efficiency is challenging our historic preoccupation with minimum standards, equality, and the pursuit of excellence. The politician of today is unimpressed with demands for more money to schools, no matter how equitable the plans for distribution of the benefits to children, or the burdens to taxpayers. The politicians want specific and quantitative information on the schools' output and on how much better the schools will be—a type of information that is not available to school officials from school records as they are now kept. Because of its importance to school management, I shall focus the rest of my remarks on this fourth set of interests of economists in education—the model of the mechanical system, the criterion of efficiency, the analytical methods of cost-benefit studies and systems analysis, and the dynamic and innovational possibilities of program planning and budgeting systems.

One can choose to dismiss this movement as a recurrence of the activities associated with the cult of efficiency that overtook school affairs half a century ago, with the unhappy effects for education outlined so vividly by Callahan in the book mentioned earlier, *Education and the Cult of Efficiency*. Or one can conclude, as I suggested earlier, that since a new priesthood is in power in Washington, we have a new catechism to learn, and so dismiss it as ritual. Indeed, I have seen evidence in recent conferences between federal and local officials that this is what is happening, for when an *appropriate* question is asked, the answer is interrupted if it is *the appropriate* answer.

However, I am inclined to think we cannot dismiss this movement lightly for three reasons: first, because this time it emerges with a much broader intellectual undergirding and logical sophistication; second, be-

cause politicians are seizing upon it as a
means for controlling school costs, which
have risen steadily throughout this century
at a rate faster than that of the total economy;
and, third, because it is a new manifestation
of mechanistic models for thinking about
human institutions, an attitude that has recurred with increasing vigor over many centuries. Therefore, I argue for knowing more
about the movement, its assumptions, its
methods, and its objectives.

* * *

A first step is to recognize that, though
the models are derived from the physical
world, they grow in complexity and perhaps
in sophistication through application to social phenomena. The simplest of the mechanistic models is the single-purpose engine
designed to do one thing, such as raising
water or transferring heat; the appropriate
research tool is cost-benefit analysis. Yet the
attempt to apply the simplest model to social
institutions, even those presumed to have
single purposes, such as food service or
transportation, introduces endless elabora-

tions. Analogies from models of more complex machines are now being made to more complex social institutions, including schools, and systems analysis is proposed as the appropriate research tool. Program planning and budgeting systems is a dynamic and hopefully predictive model; it is the most complex, even in the physical world but where it leads in the analysis of social institutions is not yet clear.

The intellectual and philosophical assumptions that underlie various approaches to the study of education and to the design of various systems and processes used in education may have far-reaching social influences. In turn, society has a reciprocal constraint on the system or process. Boguslaw, a RAND systems specialist, in his *The New Utopians: A Study of Systems Design and Social Change* (1965) distinguishes four approaches to systems design that indicate gross differences in methodology and implicit if not explicit differences in answers. These approaches are:

1. Formalist or model builders approach, including symbolic and mathematical models;

2. Heuristic or dynamic principle approach;
3. Operating unit approach, based on people, machines, or processes selected or developed to possess specific performance characteristics;
4. The Ad Hoc design based on present reality, with no commitment to models, principles, or operating units.

All four of the models I have discussed fall into the Formalist category. The typical public school, on the other hand, uses the Operating unit approach. Public school systems often become the instrument, not only for providing educational and custodial services, but also for serving many community, business, and welfare concerns in distributing employment and business contracts in ways that satisfy the community voters.

In examining the investment, production, motivation, and systems models in the light of their implied assumptions, and looking further for the probable criteria of efficiency that each would employ, I have tried to highlight the bias that each would introduce into its results. No amount of subsequent manipulation can eliminate initial biases that are imposed upon policy and program decisions by selecting a certain model as a guide to analyze performance.

For example, investment models imply a criterion measure of dollar yield to the economy and/or to individuals. This materialistic influence can become an absolute guide and be used to focus attention only on those aspects of education that are conveniently measured in materialistic terms.

The production model bias has been with us for a long time, but, without the essential ingredient of product evaluation, educationists have become much enamoured with the process and the "through-put" and less concerned with long-term measurement of the quality of the schools' output. Over the past several decades the production *process* has been perfected and refined so that from the standpoint of the idealist who reasons with the production model, we already have the best of all possible models. Since the assumption is that the process is more than adequate, if there is any deficiency in the results, the fault must lie in the quality of the input; for example, witness the complaints of school personnel about the poor quality of students they receive, and thus the need to *pre*-process the culturally deprived in order to obtain a uniform input to the unvarying educational process. And, since the process is often viewed as separable from the product and of more concern to the schools, there is no need to measure the output in any manner. The preoccupation with the process has led to ignoring any effort toward a criterion measure of the "finished goods."

Motivational models focus on the beneficiary and his presumed needs. Since these needs may not be known consciously to the individual, they must be detected and a conditioning process developed by some objective expert. The subjective problem of measuring the benefits perceived by the beneficiary, as well as the potential for hidden assumptions creeping into the manipulation of latent needs, are the aspects of this model that should be given explicit recognition.

The systems models stress the concept that multiple alternatives are to be presented to decision-makers with sufficient supporting data to assure informed decisions. What becomes critical is the acknowledgment that a myriad of prior decisions have been made throughout the process and that *all* possible alternatives can never be presented. This is to say that the decision-maker must remain aware that the totality of concrete possibilities are not explained by the model. The latter point is a reiteration of the caveat of utilizing any of the Formalist approaches: A model is an abstraction from reality, and as such cannot be generalized to all concrete situations.

*   *   *

In many parts of the county schoolmen are already engaged in some level of cost-benefit analyses on some parts of the total school operation. Such analyses are a familiar part of normal operation in many school systems, more recently in negotiating for new federal program funds (though not, I might add, without full evidence of the meeting of minds usually required in contract negotiations!). In the past, too, some fairly sophisticated cost-benefit studies were done, in such areas as transportation and food services, though often with too narrow a frame of reference and with haphazard methodology.

The purpose of cost-benefit analysis is to find a way to give the highest net value to benefits after all costs are deducted. This, I suppose, is an economist's statement of the first law of thermodynamics, or perhaps is equivalent to a scientific restatement of the Golden Rule. That it is so fundamental emphasizes our imminent danger of being saddled with a new priesthood. Usually, in application of this purpose to schools, there are constraints on achieving either highest benefits or lowest costs, such as differences of opinion about the aims of education and the purpose of life, or legally vested interests of employees and privileged classes of patrons or clientele, or disadvantages to individuals that cannot be allocated on political or humanitarian grounds. The rules of the game require that such constraints be specified, and their effects measured as accurately as possible in the process. The analysis ideally is long-range, longer than for an annual budget period, so that both costs and benefits can be estimated in their broadest possible effects and converted to annual net costs. For instance, it would be necessary, in studying cost-benefit effects of a school transportation system, to consider the alternatives of building smaller and more decentralized schools giving due regard to higher operating costs and amortization of capital and interest costs, against the economies of building fewer and larger attendance centers and thereby increasing transport costs; or to take another instance, comparing the costs and benefits (broadly defined) of transporting children of widely dispersed families living on public welfare against such an alternative as assuming the costs of having the families moved closer to the school. Higher order concerns may bring in the issues of racial, social, or economic integration. Similarly, a cost-benefit survey of food services would balance the advantages of a single food-capsule against costs of traditional programs, taking into account such constraints as food traditions, preferences, and taboos of the pupils to be served, and their attendant effects on costs and benefits.

A common difficulty with past efforts to apply cost-benefit analysis in education is that school officials let apprehensions about the constraints prevent thorough analysis; they have found it easier to suffer discomforts arising from standard operating procedures than to face the unforeseen dislocations almost sure to follow if they are changed. Furthermore, any attempt to use this analytical approach will require a much more enlightened and explicit recognition of the function of the school in our society as a custodial institution, a function that is now little discussed and only poorly understood by public and professionals alike. Thus some will argue that analysis must be done by outside agencies, such as consulting firms or university consultants. Others insist that schools not only can but must find or train staff who can analyze operations internally, as a routine part of the administrative process. Either approach is likely to be hindered by almost overwhelming pressures from both school boards and school staff to avoid controversial proposals, and any proposal for change is usually controversial.

By noting the constraints often imposed

by conservative school officials, I do not mean to minimize the constraints placed on cost-benefit analysis by the present state of the art, for admittedly it is in a primitive state. We keep it primitive by resisting any efforts to plan ahead that go beyond short extrapolations from historical trends, and by concealing our implied assumptions, such as that schools shall take over more of the custodial functions historically accepted by the family.

Critics quite rightly point out that the new techniques show no better promise for controlling the dark uncertainties that lie in our future than witchcraft, or even, perhaps, prayer. On the other hand, more careful and disciplined analyses of the state of our affairs can surely alert us more quickly to significant events as they occur, and allow us to adjust our plans more promptly to take uncertainties into account as the future unfolds them and makes them certain. The logic of successive approximations in a climate of continuous concern is very persuasive. When the techniques are mysterious, it is sensible to be suspicious about applying them, for to the extent that techniques are truly mysterious

they are probably not useful. On the other
hand, most of the new techniques are under-
standable, can be learned by the reasonably
capable man, and will take social values as
given. Many of the processes are tedious,
such as the calculation of interest rates at
various levels in estimating one of many costs
of a given course of action; yet bankers have
come to know that such calculations are not
mysterious, and they are very profitable.
School officials can share in such profitable
ventures by, for instance, calculating the costs
of purchasing school sites ten years in advance of their needs. Such calculations involve estimating the future rise in land values
in order to estimate the cost of purchase ten
years hence, and adding to the present cost
the interest charges that would accrue over
the ten-year period, the taxes that would
be foregone over the same period, and estimating the fiscal capabilities of the district
at the two points in time. This is not a
mysterious process, but is in fact a very
straightforward, quite unsophisticated, and
perhaps an oversimplified example of cost-
benefit analysis which recently saved a Cali-

fornia school district more than a million dollars. If we cultivate the habit of identifying alternative courses of action, exploring their probable consequences systematically, I am sure we can devise increasingly useful applications. I emphasize again, however, the need for long-range planning. We have become quite sophisticated in building mechanistic models to estimate the productivity of investment in urban development, for instance, but rarely have we extrapolated them to their inevitable ends of obsolescence and demolition. Had we done so the results might have alerted us to the effects of spiraling down to urban decay not attended to in the early enthusiasms of development.

The difficulties involved in attempting to quantify all dimensions of educational matters should not be allowed to obscure the benefits of trying to use these analytical aids, for even when imperfectly used they cause officials and citizens to look at problems in a systematic way. In this sense, there is at least guidance in asking the right questions.

The cost-benefit study is, as I have said before, the simplest and most essential of the analytical methods leading to the more complex systems analysis and the enormous complexities of program planning and budgeting systems. Before leaving this relatively simple tool of inquiry, I wish to emphasize again that its purpose is efficiency, to be achieved by substituting parts in a mechanical model—either by substituting less expensive but equally acceptable goals or products, or by substituting less costly materials or personnel that can serve equally well to accomplish the purposes intended. Whether this simplistic model is readily adaptable to social institutions is perhaps one of the most significant questions of our time.

*   *   *

Systems analysis becomes enormously more complex because the analyst will usually deal with a much larger set of variables, because the scale of operations is usually greater, and because he may want not only to substitute a new set of materiel or personnel input but may also arrive at an entirely new set of purposes for the system under study. For instance, a whole set of concerns about transporting, feeding, and housing school children becomes irrelevant if we devise ways of placing the necessities for pursuing an education in the home (though, admittedly, mothers might be expected to place some constraints on such a proposal). Or, to take an actual instance, plans for efficiently operating state institutions for the care and education of handicapped children, although carefully done, became irrelevant when states began to make payments to local districts (often tenfold the allotments being made for the normal child) to encourage decentralization of these programs. In spite of increases in payments, state costs went down sharply because the costs of the custodial care of these children was shifted back to the family, a shift that experience has shown to be both acceptable to the family as well as beneficial to the social integration of the children. This is one of the best examples I know to illustrate why cost-benefit analysis is best undertaken in the larger context of systems analysis where alternative systems and substitute approaches may be considered.

The importance of imagination and creative thinking in systems analysis may give us reason to worry about how much talent we can find capable of making widespread use of the technique. Here again much of the usefulness of the technique rests in the orderly and disciplined attention given to analyzing the situation surrounding a problem, to finding ways to quantify as many of the relevant variables as possible, to devising simplified models within which the variables can be manipulated, and to changing—as imagination dictates and as capacity for calculation and procurement allows—the materials, personnel, and even purposes to be achieved, in order to arrive at proposals for alternative courses of action and their consequences. The systems analyst must be free to ignore the purposes defined for the system, for his task may include an improvement in or a sharp redirection of purposes. To return again to the mechanistic model, we would have closed off a whole spectrum of experimentation if we had required our engineers to limit themselves to thinking about transportation by land and water, or even to propeller-driven crafts in the air. I am reminded also of the large volume of very bad educationist "literature" built up through the first three decades of this century on how to design, use, and control study halls; life has been simpler for all concerned in those schools that simply abandoned them.

With the study hall in mind, one may ask, how many other traditional functions are we harboring that would fall into the same category? It is the systematic review and reformulation of means and ends that challenges the rationalized traditions that may lead to the most creative advantages of program planning and budgeting systems (PPBS). For instance, in realistically examining the conditions and consequences of migration from rural areas of the country to urban centers over the past two decades educators and public officials have realized that a policy for support of education in poor rural areas is a necessity to maintain reasonable levels of educational attainment in the urban centers. Further, the state and local money invested in the education of young people in those states from which rural migrants come warrants reimbursement to the extent that the investment in education that is drained away exceeds the returned benefits. In a program at the federal level a policy for support of education in those depressed areas becomes an explicit and highly rational alternative.

* * *

Program planning and budgeting systems have been the most complex and, to educators generally, the most disturbing of the new lines of inquiry in education. Because of its dynamic and predictive purpose, PPBS is the most complex adaptation of mechanical models to the analysis of social institutions. I suppose the main reason PPBS has so upset school officials is that it changes their perception of the school as a stable, static organization with its solid objectives rooted in its history of past performance, their view of the future as an orderly and conservative projection by extrapolation into the future. By contrast, the rules of PPBS are intended to break with the past and to force planners into a sometimes frightening future orientation, where objectives may change markedly, technology may be substituted for human effort, and existing institutional arrangements are almost certain to become irrelevant, have in fact in many instances already become in part irrelevant.

PPBS has powerful support at the federal level, and increasing support at the state level as well. With the emphasis on PPBS approaches imbedded in the Elementary and Secondary Education Act of 1965, it cannot be ignored at either state or local levels. We may expect information produced through the PPBS to increase at all levels of government; and it is upon this kind of information that legislative decisions about schools will be made, which may very well change the aims of education, and the schools as well.

Perhaps the new approaches to budgeting and planning are best illustrated by contrasting their aims, their processes, and their effects on organizations with those of older methods. Traditional school budgeting and accounting is prudential, designed to safeguard the public monies, and to make an historical and accountable record to show that money was spent as intended when voted. The process in traditional budgeting is incremental; the budget for each period starts from the base of the previous period, and attention focuses on the amounts of change in the budget categories for the next period. This approach is essentially conservative, since the largest proportion of the budget, usually in excess of 90 percent, projects the school system into the new period with much the same plan as in the previous period.

The conventional budget presents decision-makers only with an outline of expenditures for personnel, equipment and materials, and other input categories. The decision-maker is faced with the task of extrapolating from these input aggregates into the individual ongoing programs. The decision-maker must create an image in his mind of how the pieces of the budget are to be conjoined to form a working system. The interrelationships between programs are especially difficult to envision. Any reduction in a total category, in the absence of specific directives, means that administrative decisions have to be made as to how this reduction will affect specific programs.

A further shortcoming of annual budgeting

is that it encourages preoccupation with the next fiscal year, which tends to encourage foot-in-the-door techniques. This latter approach involves a small budget outlay for the initial stage of operating a "pilot" program. Such programs have a way of becoming permanent and require increasingly greater allocations in subsequent years.

Incrementalism has evolved in the traditional budgetary process as a systematic analytical procedure for determining educational policy. It involves a series of successive approximations chosen by comparing a limited number of alternatives and evaluating these alternatives in relation to the preceived values held by the schools' service area. By revising the policy goals in accord with what is learned about social values, incrementalism moves gradually toward an improved position.

In contrast, PPBS is innovative; attention is focused on choosing from many possible objectives those specific objectives to be achieved, and then choosing from alternate courses of action that plan which will accomplish the chosen objectives at the lowest

possible cost, or accomplish some more opti-
mum set of objectives at a specified cost.
The process is comprehensive in that it re-
quires each budget to be built from a zero
base, not from the previous base. The approach encourages change because at least
the possibility exists that an organization will
be altered substantially each time a budget is
made. It is no wonder that school officials
find PPBS disturbing; given lifelong exposure
to the conservative climate of the school,
which is one of the most stable institutions
in our society, they find it difficult to cope
with the potential for change inherent in this
new budget procedure.

Yet it is precisely the stability of schools
that is now under attack in our society, for
evidence accumulates that schools are out
of joint with the times. One hears that the
social purposes schools are expected to accomplish are not being accomplished, or are
being accomplished less efficiently or less ef-
fectively than is desirable. The unsettled
question remains: are we hearing the demand for services to advance social purposes,
or to advance more narrowly defined pur-

poses serving the burgeoning technocracy seeking markets in education?

We must also look at the types of decisions to be made. Most educational decisions seem to be a selection from multiple possibilities with very little gradation to distinguish the "good" from the "not so good" choices. Sophisticated techniques may be little more efficient here than the individual's value judgment. A less frequent decision situation is one in which one choice is clearly preferable to the rest of the set, and rule-of-thumb devices can be employed, almost routinely, to make nearly optimal decisions. Educators often artificially force decisions into the clear choice pattern by assuming major constraints which exclude alternatives. An example of this is the narrowly restricted concept held by many school administrators of what is the "proper" role of the schools: that the functions to be performed are simply and exclusively the three R's. We then find that the total educational process is dysfunctional because the formal program has ignored the sometime competing educational influences of the family, neighborhood, and community.

It is possible that PPBS may encourage us to acknowledge and integrate our activities with those of the larger community and with the entire range of educational agencies. Considerable benefit may accrue merely by correcting the myopic viewpoints of many educators.

The meaning of "program budgeting" has come rapidly to include a number of administrative and technical processes. It may mean only the utilization of an output or program-oriented budget format, or it may involve the program budget format *plus* cost-benefit analysis to guide decisions either on an informal, ad hoc basis, or on a formal institutionalized basis.

In institutions where the budgeting function is already established on a traditional basis, or if there are legal or other restrictions on altering the budget categories, it may be possible to engage in a programming process as an intermediate step. Programming in this sense would translate the traditional categories of the input-oriented budget into regrouped program categories. Such reformulation of proposed and actual expenditures would assist proper analysis, especially forward planning. Since the programming process as an intermediate step involves an extra process, it would be theoretically ideal to convert budgeting to a program basis. With the intermediate step, moreover, the legal constraints on accounting and budgeting formats so common to state school systems are not insuperable barriers to PPBS.

Program budget categories cut across the traditional classifications and reflect "assembled packages" of men, material, and equipment that comprise an operating entity with a specific objective. The program-oriented budget has certain advantages over the traditional input budget. The program format enables decision-makers to focus their attention on the alternatives available to them to shift resources from one program to another. When the program budget is accompanied by cost-benefit data to support the various alternatives, choices can be made by weighing the gains from each proposal against the costs and foregone opportunities. The factor of the potential "trade-offs" is considered by many to be the major virtue of program budgeting. This is not to deny the existence of informal bargaining and trading under conventional systems; but it should be noted that such bargaining was often undertaken at lower levels and became embedded in the program by tacit agreement. The cost-benefit estimates that accompany program alternatives are presented as full-cost projections that include both initial costs and probable future costs. The full cost estimates tend to thwart the foot-in-the-door game and enable decisions to be made on a more informed basis.

As used in systems design and computer programming, a contemporary connotation of *heuristic* is an approach to decision-making that utilizes operationally stated principles, or even hunches, which provide directions or guides to problem-solvers faced with a completely novel or unanticipated situation. These guides for action are only first approximations and are not considered infallible laws; in this sense they are quite different from the "principles" so exhaustively taught over the past half century. In education we often utilize simple rules of thumb, such as always selecting the middle range of expenditures, rejecting those on the high and low ends of the continuum; or in contract bids we may consider only those at the lower end. Thus, in an emergent situation, this heuristic approach would provide a prescription for action in making purchasing or hiring decisions. Or we may have more complex heuristics which verge on ideological principles and pervade much of our decision-making, such as the rugged individualist's belief that increased competition will cure most school budget problems.

Difficulties arise when heuristics remain static while situations are shifting. The sorting of students into college prep and vocational tracks on a fixed ratio may have merit in efficiently utilizing educational facilities and manpower at one stage of a nation's economic development, but may be quite inappropriate when the country attains a higher level of development, or when technology is increasing so rapidly that the emergent situations are making vocational skills obsolete at high rates.

It seems to be inevitable that rules of

thumb will be used to guide complex decision-making. We seldom have the opportunity to reach optimally perfect decisions; therefore, we are content with viable solutions that approach or exceed reasonable standards. Herbert Simon's concept of "satisficing" represents the level of decision-making we can economically hope to attain. Systems analysts and experts generally tend to impose different (in their minds, "better") decision rules than management has been using, but these are still rules of thumb.

A number of writers have noted that the collective effect of bargaining and trading by individuals, politicians, and voters operates like an unseen hand to constrain each individual and to guide decisions. The unseen hand of compromise parallels the influence of the "invisible hand" of Adam Smith's free market economy. It has been argued that PPBS may be a means of institutionalizing change as long as it permits controversial programs to be reviewed publicly on a regular basis. It can permit the unseen hand of negotiation and bargaining to achieve some balance in the overall program.

The ultimate usefulness of PPBS will be determined by the way in which it becomes embedded in our institutions. The PPBS approach itself should be subjected to cost-benefit analysis and its relative merits should be weighed by the appropriate level of decision-makers before the concept is accepted or rejected. The success of the system will depend on the situational variables: the degree of legitimation it is afforded; the manner in which it is integrated into the organizational structure; and the way the components are phased into operation. In this sense, the success of the endeavor will be contingent upon a careful analysis of the organizational context within which it will operate.

A program budgeting system intrinsically has slight impact on incentives to provide and use information. If program budgeting is considered little more than a communication device, it will undoubtedly result in no more than a new way to shuffle papers. There is speculation that the success of PPBS at the federal level would have had little effect if it had not been linked with shifts in authority.

It would be improper to attribute a causal effect between the adoption of program budgeting and such shifts of power, but it may be necessary to provide administrative centralization to make the PPBS process effective. This is one of the aspects of PPBS that should be weighed in advance, and is now being weighed in states where the decisions have already been made to use the authority of the state to accomplish the change in local school districts.

At a minimum, the organizational structure should be modified when PPBS is undertaken to build in a formal mechanism to encourage and review changes to programs. In order to keep the system dynamic, program change proposals should be submitted periodically, especially if long-range planning is involved. I will comment later on some practical reorganizations of local administrative arrangements to speed the change.

* * *

Part of the difficulty in getting the new approach started in local schools lies in the speed with which school officials are being propelled into the world of PPBS, which assumes familiarity with cost-benefit studies and the more complex systems analyses. We find ourselves in the plight of a student plunged into algebra before he has learned to do arithmetic. In the past our budgets focused on the needs of an organization which we projected forward conservatively from historical roots; social institutions do not make long jumps around sharp corners to places that cannot be seen. Hopefully, however, they should be capable of coping with future events. PPBS directs our attention to the innovative task of anticipating, inventing, and planning for future events and designing the organization necessary to bring them into being and to manage them.

The PPBS supporters acknowledge that the concept is not without shortcomings, some of which have to do with the state of the art and lack of qualified personnel to administer it, and some of which are inherent in the system. The prime hope is that the methodology and the analytical tools will, in and of themselves, provide considerable benefit to the users. It is easy, however, to oversell prospective users on the amount of useful information that program budgeting will generate. In education, where we are just now learning to state teaching objectives explicitly, we are forced under program budgeting to deal with far more subtle objectives—many of which have never been stated explicitly.

Although the consideration of relevant trade-offs is one of the principal advantages of PPBS, it is recognized that, whichever set of program or input categories is combined to focus on a particular activity, that set constrains the analyst and leads away from looking at other combinations. We may tend to think of one way of combining activities as "better" than others which automatically excludes all other possible combinations and permutations. Related to this problem is the difficulty of spotlighting interrelationships and interdependencies between programs. Even though a systematic approach will explicate many interconnections, the modification of one program may have unintended consequences, or what are termed "ricochet effects," on related programs.

The quantification and evaluation of programs on budget exhibits may be somewhat misleading unless two caveats are observed: (1) criteria of effectiveness are quite limited, and (2) program costs are based on estimates of variable accuracy. The orderly mathematical procedures of cost-benefit analysis tend to give a spurious degree of certainty to the decision-maker when, in fact, contingencies often make realization of goals uncertain. The conditional aspects are due in part to the incommensurables and uncertainties which are necessarily encompassed in developing programs. These contingencies, however, do not preclude handling the variables in a systematic and explicit manner. The federal advocates of PPBS have conceded that it may be impossible in many situations to find a single, conceptually clear output measure. The argument on "standards" for judging effectiveness is one that has been with education for centuries. We often employ proxy indexes of efficiency at a given point in time which are subject to considerable improvement over time, such as equating higher teacher salaries with higher teacher effectiveness.

There has been some criticism of PPBS by those who feel that any highly ordered bureaucratic approach is antithetical to creativity and innovation. This line of criticism is related to the school of thought that believes that creative and divergent outcomes are possible only through inspirational and fortuitous acts. This thinking ignores the possibility of deliberate programming of research and development allocations so as to build them into the system on a flexible, delegative basis rather than on the basis of by-the-formula specificity. This criticism also appears to confuse styles of leadership with the process employed.

A critical problem that has not been fully explored is which *forums* will best serve the final decision-makers. In nonmarket decision-making we can use some of the more rigorous econometric procedures to provide us with some conception of which trade-offs will be optimal, but it is apparent that the alternatives that favor some persons without wronging others—that is, the so-called "Pareto" optimal alternatives—are few in number. But, even from the set of Pareto optimal actions, some mechanism must be employed to select the trade-off that is best for all concerned.

Centralized decision-making is one way of selecting the best alternative from the set of feasible and desirable alternatives. Here, expert judgment provides a valid guide to obtaining the proper choice. The case for central decision assumes that the decision-maker can locate the underlying value premise that determines the content of public opinion in a given situation. Central decision-making in a bureaucratic framework is effective in handling routine and relatively harmonious tasks. Central goals and an internal unity maintained by selective recruiting and socialization are combined to achieve conformity and equilibrium. Centralization admittedly has its drawbacks. It makes the resultant course of action dependent upon one set of attitudes, values, and norms, removes some of the incentives for lower echelons to be concerned with choices, and increases the burdens of top management.

According to those who view conflict as functional to the central social process, conflict and competing ideas over goals and means are more characteristic of the real world. What PPBS can do is provide a vehicle for bringing together diverse social and ideological groups if the final decision-making forum is in some way representative of these diverse forces. Since we are constantly searching for ways to bring the common man into the decision-making process in a democracy, we may use elected representatives, such as the elected school boards, to convert the desires of the electorate into decision-making. This social-choice case rests on the distribution and amount of political influence which can be exercised in behalf of various alternatives in a continuing game of bargaining and exchange. A multiplicity of judgments tends to avoid a single bias and is a hedge against mistakes in judgment. The pluralistic approach also forms a system of checks and balances against prejudiced officials and tyrannical majorities. Undoubtedly, there are many situations in which it would be important to combine both central decision-making and the social forum approaches in a mixed decision-choice process. In those situations in which the complexity of the problem is great and relevant values and criteria of effectiveness are not known, it would appear that the social-choice process will produce a greater range of alternatives and a more realistic analysis of these alternatives than central decision-making. What is suggested in the forum is advocacy approaches to decision-making, not adversary proceedings before a mediating body. Unfortunately, in these latter years school boards have tended toward mediation in adversary hearings.

* * *

One may ask, what are the practical steps that a given local school system might take to organize itself in ways that will speed the development of more sophisticated approaches to budget planning?

The first step, and one that is generalizable to other areas of the large district operation, is to make more explicit than schools generally do now the need for specialization of school personnel. The widespread practice of line promotion on a seniority basis has had a deadly effect on all school operations including business management of district af-

fairs. The account clerk, or bookkeeper, or
business teacher who learns the necessary
routines and then progresses upward through
various district ratings of accountant and
business manager positions is not likely to
emerge at age sixty as the ideal innovator
for program planning and budgeting systems. I have examined much of the literature
generated by professional meetings of school
business officials in this decade, and it indi-
cates an increasing awareness of, and indeed
interest in, the impending revolution in
school management that the new techniques
portend. Furthermore, a national study of
program budgeting reported at the 1967
meeting of the Association of School Business
Officials of the United States and Canada
stressed general agreement that these innovations would be an improvement over traditional budgeting procedures, techniques, and
formats, and that they would require "more
as well as highly trained personnel and an
increased need for electronic data processing." They also recognized the probability
that these innovations would tend to further
centralize many educational decisions at

state and national levels, and that a "genuine possibility exists that the work being done by experts in accounting, data processing, and systems analysis may lead to the development of a program budgeting system for public education, including educational program structure and measurements of program effectiveness, without the leadership and active participation of outstanding leaders in the educational profession." The surprising thing was that, though they expressed concern, the principal proposal was for cooperation in development of a uniform state plan for a uniform system of program budgeting (which is a conflict in terms) and in the process "caution should be exercised not to proceed too rapidly"![5]

The business managers are probably correct in their expectation that experts in accounting, data processing, and systems analysis will develop PPBS without the leadership of what they call "educational leaders," because in this instance these leaders

[5] Association of School Business Officials of the United States and Canada, *Proceedings* (Evanston, Illinois, 1967), pp. 161–62.

are indeed not proceeding too rapidly. If we assume this prediction is correct, then we might prepare ourselves for living with the new circumstances by preparing an appropriate administrative structure to house the new capabilities.

A first step is to recognize a fundamental separation of business management and accounting functions from forward planning of programs and budget systems. This can be accomplished organizationally by creating an administrative unit reporting directly to the superintendent in a line separated from both business administration and administration of instruction, with all of the research, data processing, and operations analysis capabilities of the district included in it.

Let the budget unit be charged with defining and redefining viable subsystems within the district and with prescribing the forms in which accounts are kept in the business and accounting unit so that information is organized in ways best suited to pursuing analysis of the operations. Let it be charged with preparation of both short- and long-range plans for alternative ways of managing the subsystems, with the alternatives always including contracting with other agencies or corporations for services. Specifications for staffing the budget and planning unit should be carefully drawn not to provide positions for existing personnel, for they will doubtless continue to be needed in their present positions, but to attract the best possible talent in analysts, cost accountants, and broadly oriented and well-prepared administrators with expertise and experience in both instructional and fiscal management. Let the school board and the superintendent face the fact that this unit would contain some of the most expensive talent employed by the district, but that its cost might be comparable in the short run with that of employing a firm of management consultants for a general survey, and that in the long run the cost-benefit ratio probably would favor establishing the permanent district unit. The kind of talent needed for such a unit is now being developed in many places, including university programs; we are, for instance, launching at Stanford this year a joint program involving the Schools of Education and Business to prepare a few carefully selected individuals each year through a coordinated program leading to the degrees of Master of Business Administration and Doctor of Education, who will be well qualified to support or direct budget planning units in large school systems.

If business officials now in place can see no other advantage to such a unit as I propose, they at least should recognize that it would provide them with a place to shift any blame that now falls on them for shortcomings in school operations, and so allow them to serve out their careers in relative peace.

If any further spur to action is needed, it can be found in the recommendation of the Committee for Economic Development in its recent policy statement called "Innovation in Education: New Directions for the American School":

We urge immediate exploration by school administrators of the application of program accounting techniques in order to identify costs in school systems and to take advantage of cost comparisons. The adoption of such techniques by school districts will be advanced greatly if assistance and leadership in this area are provided by state departments of education and by university schools of business, economics, and education. In applying cost-effectiveness analysis over the whole range of school investments and costs, we urge school districts to explore thoroughly the possible benefits that will result if the use of school facilities is extended by various means to include periods during which they are now unused.

We strongly recommend that broad-based studies be made of the costs and benefits that can be expected if the various technologies involving audiovisual equipment, television, computers, and other devices are applied to instruction in the schools on a wide scale. Such studies should take into account the benefits that may be obtained through increasing the effectiveness of the learning process at the same time that they weigh the effects of the new resources in terms of the organization of instruction, teacher pay schedules, productivity, probable use by teachers, and other vital matters.[6]

This influential group, which distributes its publications to an audience that is likewise influential and remarkably attentive, has added impetus to the already pervasive demands for improving our system of decision-making in education.

[6] (New York: The Committee, 1968), p. 19.

PPBS is probably not a panacea for all the ailments of the school. On the other hand, I think it would be unwise to dismiss it either as a passing fad, or simply as a tool of management. It offers a systematic method for increasing knowledge about the structures, functions, and objectives of government services, including schools. That knowledge in turn can increase the understanding of policy-makers, and thereby increase their effectiveness in decision-making. It should improve administration and planning for the future especially in the larger units of local and state systems of education. However, educators at the local level who continue to pay little attention to redirecting their purposes and planning will simply be eliminated from consequential decisions if present trends toward centralization and purposive redirection of educational institutions continue. A disciplined way to understanding is a source of very great power in a democracy, perhaps the only one we should trust in the long run. We seem to be building a disciplined way of understanding around PPBS, and if educators want to be involved in the important policy discussions, they will need to learn the language in which much of these discussions are now conducted.

On the other hand, I argue also for humanists to build an informed case against the mechanistic model for analysis of social institutions. We are, after all, attempting to re-create our social world, and especially our schools, to fit a model of our invention. We reason that since we have created complex machines, we can now use the laws we have derived from that experience to reconstruct our social institutions. In that effort we may violate two laws of logic: (1) we may apply our mechanical model to concerns too broad to be encompassed, in the instances where we fail to perceive the proper scope of the human condition; and (2) we may apply our model to inconsequential ends when we attempt to analyze less encompassing statements of human aims.

The final argument for maintaining a wary dialogue between humanist and social planner is the failure of the mechanistic models to perform in a predictive sense when applied to human behavior in any way comparable to their capabilities in the physical world. One can argue that given full control of the minds of men to make them reason within the mechanistic model, this failure could be overcome, but the prospect of such control will add weight to the argument for the dialogue.